# UNITED STATES
# MAZE CRAZE

## VIKI WOODWORTH

## DOVER PUBLICATIONS, INC.
### MINEOLA, NEW YORK

## Note

What better way to travel through and learn about the United States than to complete fifty challenging mazes? From Alabama to Wyoming—yes, the states appear in alphabetical order—you will see the astounding variety of famous places and people from all over the country. And there's a surprise waiting at the end of each maze trail: the state capital!

As you complete the mazes, you'll find many fascinating facts, such as the location of the Gateway Arch, the home of the Cowboy Hall of Fame, and the place where Hoodoo rock formations can be visited. In addition, you'll discover the states where famous national monuments can be found, as well as the official birds for all fifty states. In some cases, a person who was born in one state is pictured on another state's page because he or she grew up there or spent more time there. Just get your pencil ready, and go from START to END in each puzzle. Solutions are included, beginning on page 51, but don't peek until you've tried your hardest to solve the mazes. When you're finished, you can have even more fun by coloring in the pages. Enjoy your amazing journey through the United States!

*Copyright*

Copyright © 2009 by Dover Publications, Inc.
All rights reserved.

*Bibliographical Note*

*United States Maze Craze* is a new work, first published by
Dover Publications, Inc., in 2009.

*International Standard Book Number*

*ISBN-13: 978-0-486-46831-0*
*ISBN-10: 0-486-46831-3*

Manufactured in the United States by Courier Corporation
46831305    2014
www.doverpublications.com

# Alabama
## The Yellowhammer State

Vulcan-IronMan-Birmingham

Moundville

Rosa Parks

Sweet Potato Pie

Cotton

start

Montgomery
☆
end

The Space Museum

Yellowhammer

·state Bird·

Pecans

Creek Tobacco Pipe

Ghost Crabs

Gees Bend Quilts

1

# Alaska
## The Last Frontier State

Skagway

Mount McKinley

Bush Planes

Caribou

Totem Poles

Inuit

Start

Gold

Salmon

Juneau ☆ end

Puffins

Sourdough Bread

King Crab

Willow Ptarmigan

Iditarod Race

·State Bird·

RED ONION SALOON

# Arizona
## The Grand Canyon State

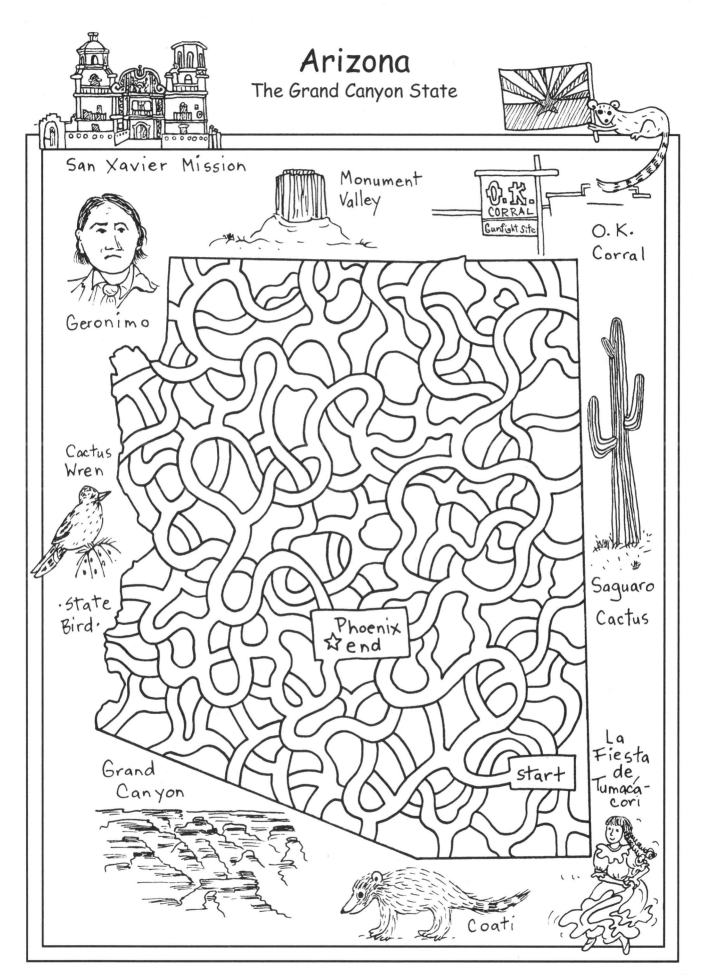

San Xavier Mission

Monument Valley

O.K. CORRAL Gunfight Site

O.K. Corral

Geronimo

Cactus Wren

·State Bird·

Phoenix ☆end

Saguaro Cactus

Grand Canyon

start

La Fiesta de Tumacacori

Coati

3

# Arkansas
## The Natural State

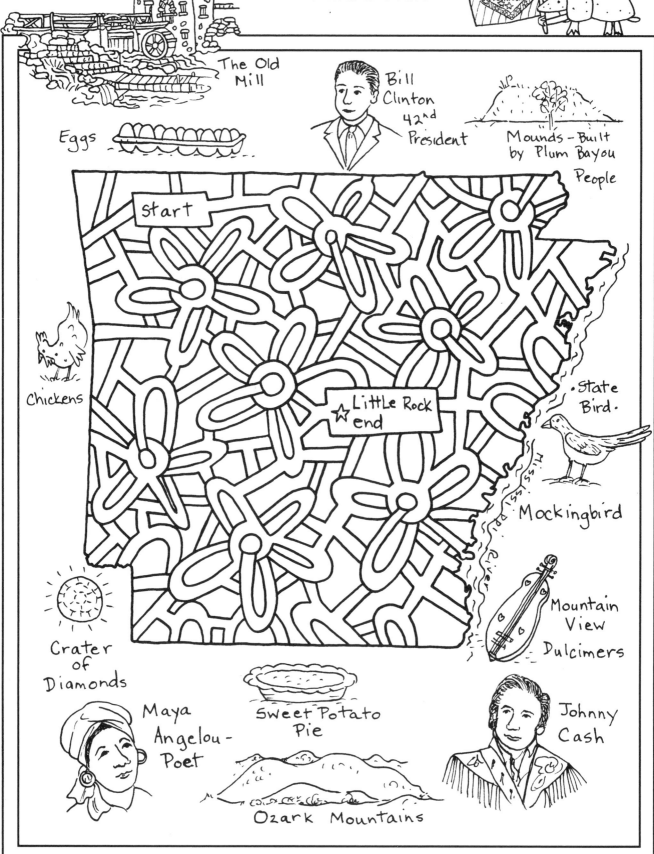

The Old Mill

Eggs

Bill Clinton 42nd President

Mounds – Built by Plum Bayou People

Start

Chickens

Little Rock end

State Bird.

Mockingbird

Mountain View Dulcimers

Crater of Diamonds

Maya Angelou – Poet

Sweet Potato Pie

Ozark Mountains

Johnny Cash

# California
## The Golden State

Mission San Carlos Borromeo del Rio Carmelo

Golden Gate Bridge

Chumash Indian Cave Art

California Valley Quail
• State Bird •

Levi's® Jeans

Gold!

Joshua Tree National Park

Sacramento end ☆

Lombard Street

Sequoia National Park

Disneyland

Hollywood

Start

5

# Colorado
## The Centennial State

Bent's Old Fort

Rocky Mountains

"The Crow"

Jim Beckwourth

Miner's Burro

U.S. Mint

Denver
☆ end

Start

Anasazi Cliff Palace

Tea

Chief Ouray

state Bird.

Lark Bunting

"Baby Doe" Tabor

Ghost Towns

# Connecticut
## The Constitution State

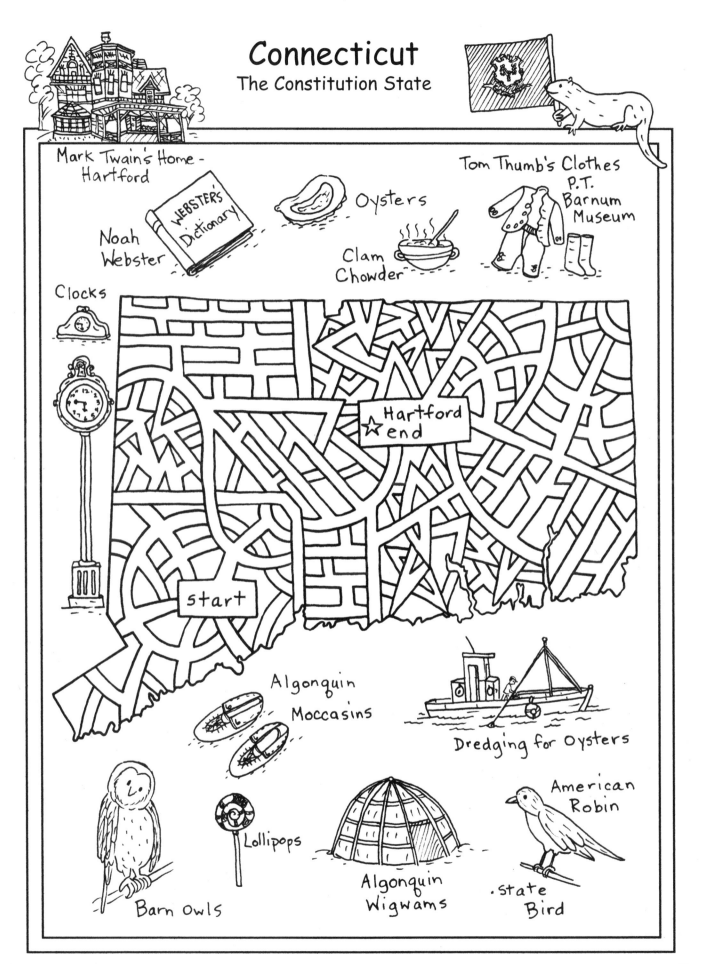

Mark Twain's Home - Hartford

Noah Webster — WEBSTER'S Dictionary

Oysters

Clam Chowder

Tom Thumb's Clothes — P.T. Barnum Museum

Clocks

Hartford end ☆

start

Algonquin Moccasins

Dredging for Oysters

Barn owls

Lollipops

Algonquin Wigwams

American Robin

.state Bird

# Delaware
## The First State

Old Swede's Church

Fenwick Island
Mason and Dixon Line Marker

Diamondback Terrapin

Henry Hudson

Lenape Indians

First DuPont Powder Mills

DuPont Chemical

☆Dover end

Start

State Bird.

Blue Hen Chicken

Caesar Rodney

The Delaware Water Gap

Horseshoe Crab

8

# Florida
## The Sunshine State

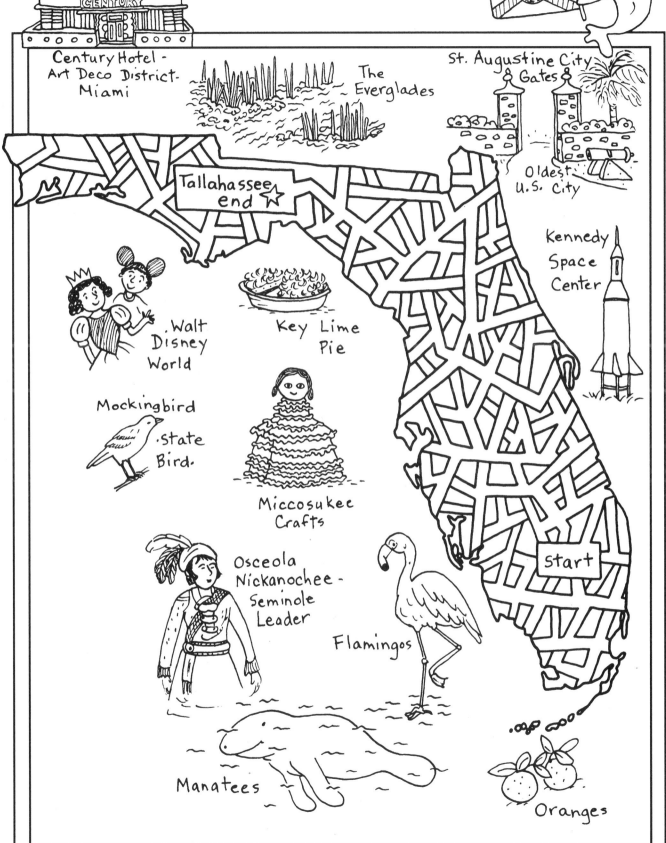

Century Hotel - Art Deco District - Miami

The Everglades

St. Augustine City Gates

Oldest U.S. City

Kennedy Space Center

Tallahassee end ★

Walt Disney World

Key Lime Pie

Mockingbird

State Bird

Miccosukee Crafts

Osceola Nickanochee - Seminole Leader

Flamingos

Start

Manatees

Oranges

9

# Georgia
## The Peach State

The Gingerbread House - Savannah

Grits

Okefenokee Swamp

Alligators

Peaches

Martin Luther King Jr.

Atlanta end ☆

Peanuts

start

Etowah Carvings

State Bird

Brown Thrasher

Shrimp

Cotton

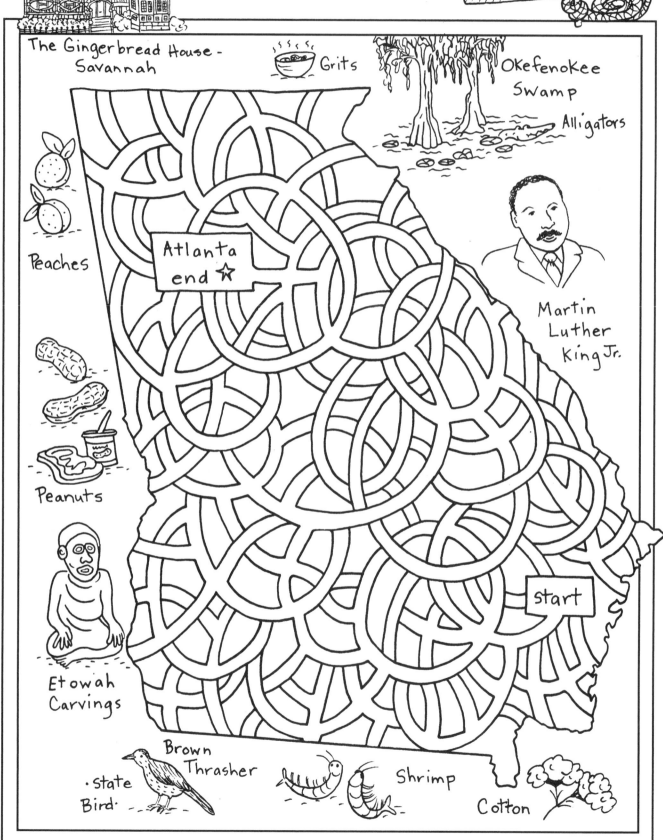

# Hawaii
## The Aloha State

State Capital Building
Honolulu

Nene · State Bird.

Spam®

Leis

Pineapples

King Kalakaua

Volcanoes

end Honolulu

Palm Trees

Early Hawaiian Houses

Ukuleles

Hula Hoops

Macadamia Nuts

Queen L'iliuokalani

Start

Hula Dancers

Sugar Cane

# Idaho
## The Gem State

Cataldo Mission

Sawtooth Mountains

~ Redfish Lake

start

Mountain Bluebird · State Bird ·

Potatoes

Soda Springs Geyser

Pictographs · Rock Drawings

Sacagawea

Lewis and Clark

Chief Joseph · Nez Perce

☆ Boise end

Star Garnets

# Illinois
## The Prairie State

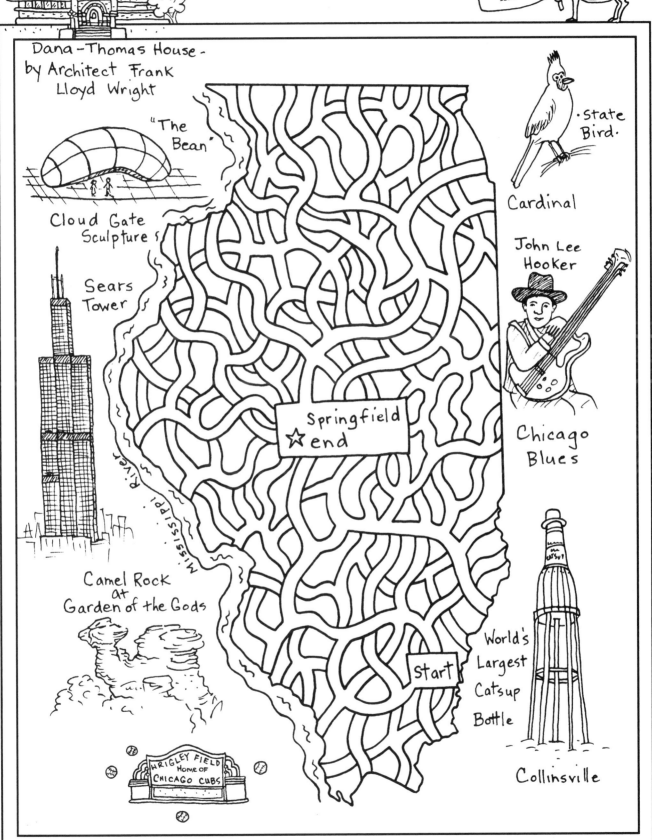

Dana-Thomas House - by Architect Frank Lloyd Wright

"The Bean"

Cloud Gate Sculpture

Sears Tower

Mississippi River

Camel Rock at Garden of the Gods

WRIGLEY FIELD HOME OF CHICAGO CUBS

Springfield ☆end

Start

State Bird.

Cardinal

John Lee Hooker

Chicago Blues

World's Largest Catsup Bottle

Collinsville

# Indiana
## The Hoosier State

The Levi Coffin House-
Underground
Railroad

Indianapolis
500

Katie
Coffin

·State
Bird·

Cardinal

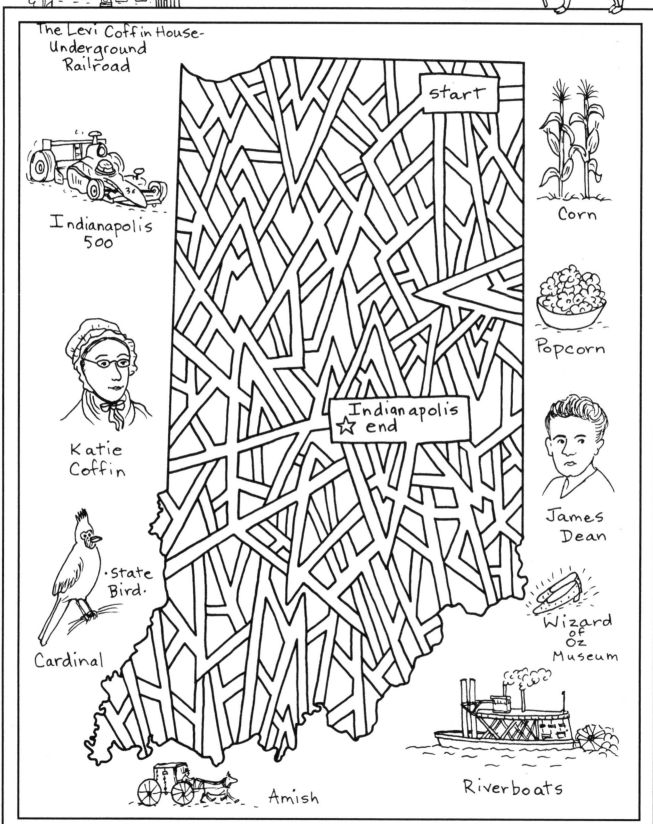

start

Indianapolis
☆ end

Corn

Popcorn

James
Dean

Wizard
of
Oz
Museum

Riverboats

Amish

# Iowa
## The Hawkeye State

Danish Windmill-
Elk Horn

Corn

Cows

Goldfinch

Farms

Pigs

·state
Bird·

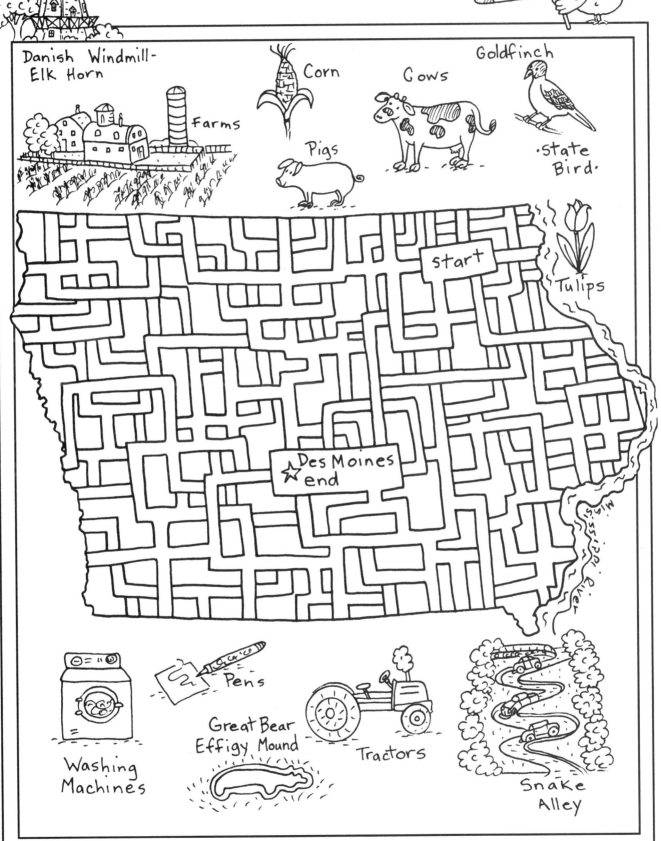

Start

Tulips

Des Moines
end

Mississippi River

Washing
Machines

Pens

Great Bear
Effigy Mound

Tractors

Snake
Alley

# Kansas
## The Sunflower State

1880's Dodge City-
Boot Hill Museum

Amelia
Earhart

Airplanes

Sunflowers

World's
Largest
Ball
of
Twine

Cawker City

State Bird.

Meadowlark

start

★ Topeka
end

Rock
City

International
Pancake
Derby

Tornadoes

Russell Stover
Chocolates

Wizard
of
Oz

# Kentucky
## The Bluegrass State

Calumet Horse Farm

Abraham Lincoln

Daniel Boone

The Hatfields and McCoys

Crafts

Frankfort ☆ end

Start

state Bird.

First Cheeseburger

Kentucky Cardinal

Shaker Furniture

Kentucky Derby

Bluegrass Music

Mammoth Caves

# Louisiana
## The Pelican State

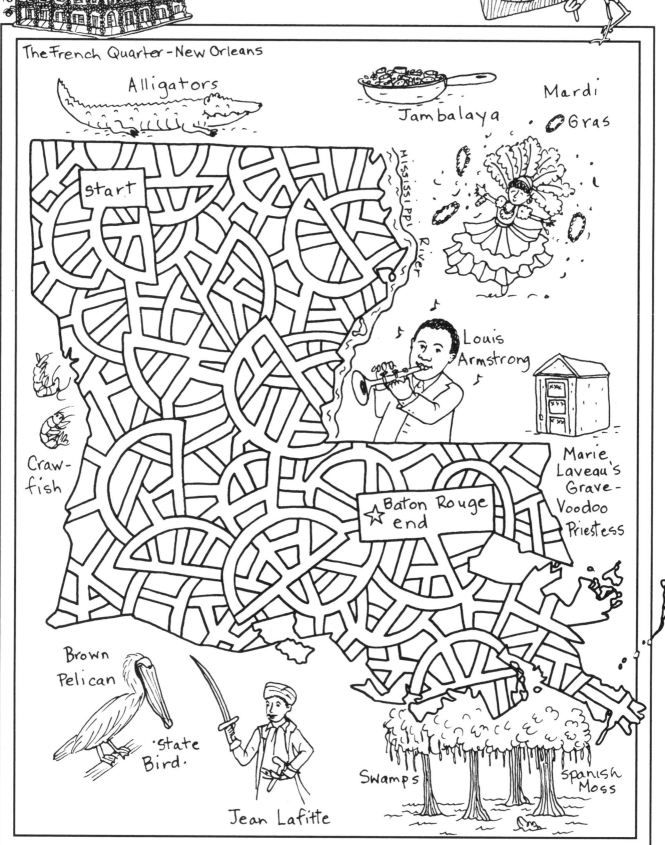

The French Quarter - New Orleans

Alligators

Jambalaya

Mardi Gras

start

MISSISSIPPI River

Louis Armstrong

Marie Laveau's Grave - Voodoo Priestess

Craw-fish

★ Baton Rouge end

Brown Pelican

·State Bird·

Jean Lafitte

Swamps

Spanish Moss

# Maine
## The Pine Tree State

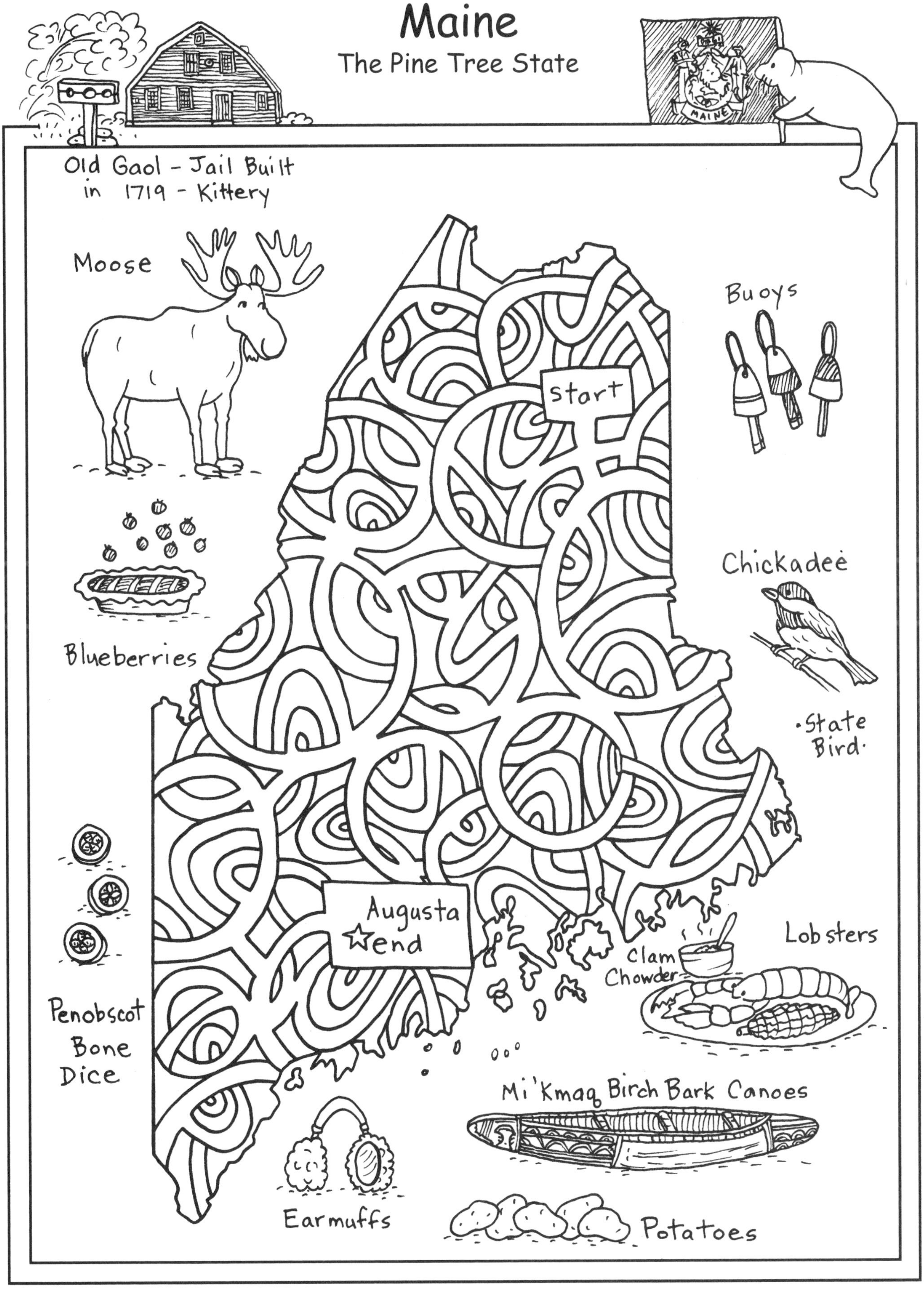

Old Gaol - Jail Built in 1719 - Kittery

Moose

Buoys

Start

Chickadee

Blueberries

·State Bird·

Augusta ☆end

Lobsters

Clam Chowder

Penobscot Bone Dice

Mi'Kmaq Birch Bark Canoes

Earmuffs

Potatoes

# Maryland
## The Old Line State

Government House

Mason-Dixon Line

Babe Ruth

• State Bird •

Baltimore Oriole

Wild Ponies Assateague Island

Start

Blue Crabs

Annapolis end

skipjacks

Harriet Tubman

Chesapeake Bay Bridge

Delmarva Fox Squirrel

Frederick Douglass

# Massachusetts
## The Bay State

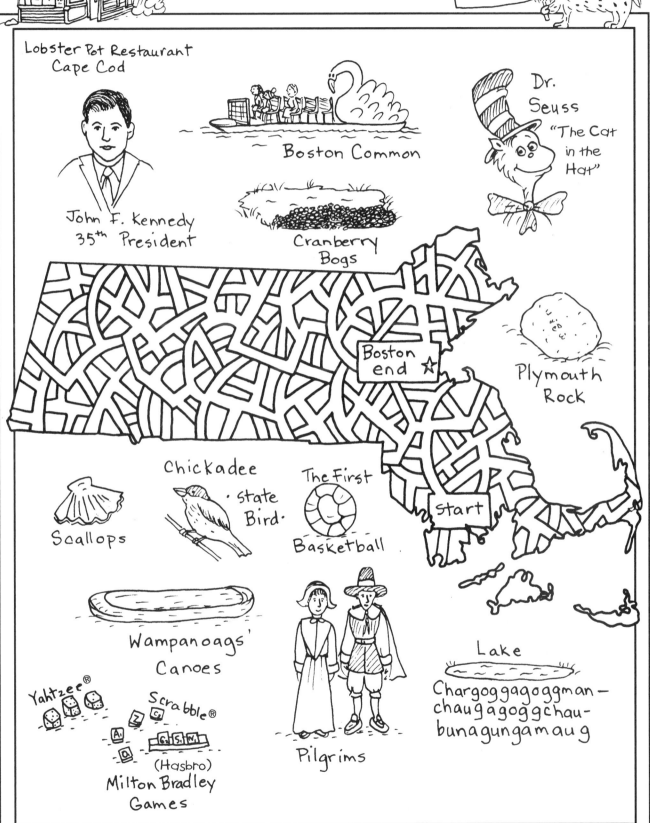

Lobster Pot Restaurant
Cape Cod

John F. Kennedy
35th President

Boston Common

Cranberry Bogs

Dr. Seuss
"The Cat in the Hat"

Boston end ☆

Plymouth Rock

Scallops

Chickadee
· State Bird ·

The First Basketball

Start

Wampanoags' Canoes

Pilgrims

Lake Chargoggagoggmanchaugagoggchaubunagungamaug

Yahtzee®

Scrabble®

(Hasbro)
Milton Bradley Games

# Michigan
## The Great Lakes State

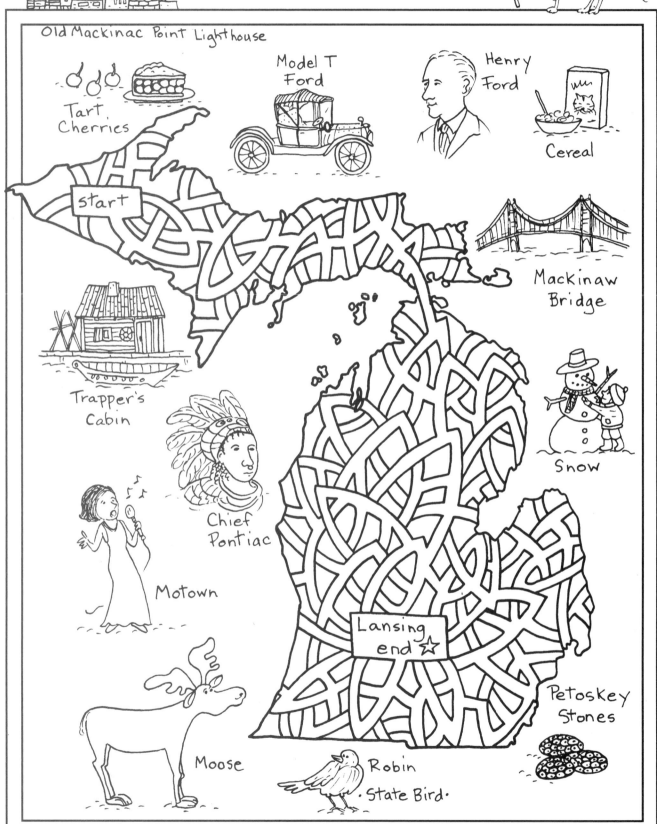

Old Mackinac Point Lighthouse

Tart Cherries

Model T Ford

Henry Ford

Cereal

start

Trapper's Cabin

Mackinaw Bridge

Snow

Chief Pontiac

Motown

Lansing end ☆

Petoskey Stones

Moose

Robin
State Bird

# Minnesota
## The North Star State

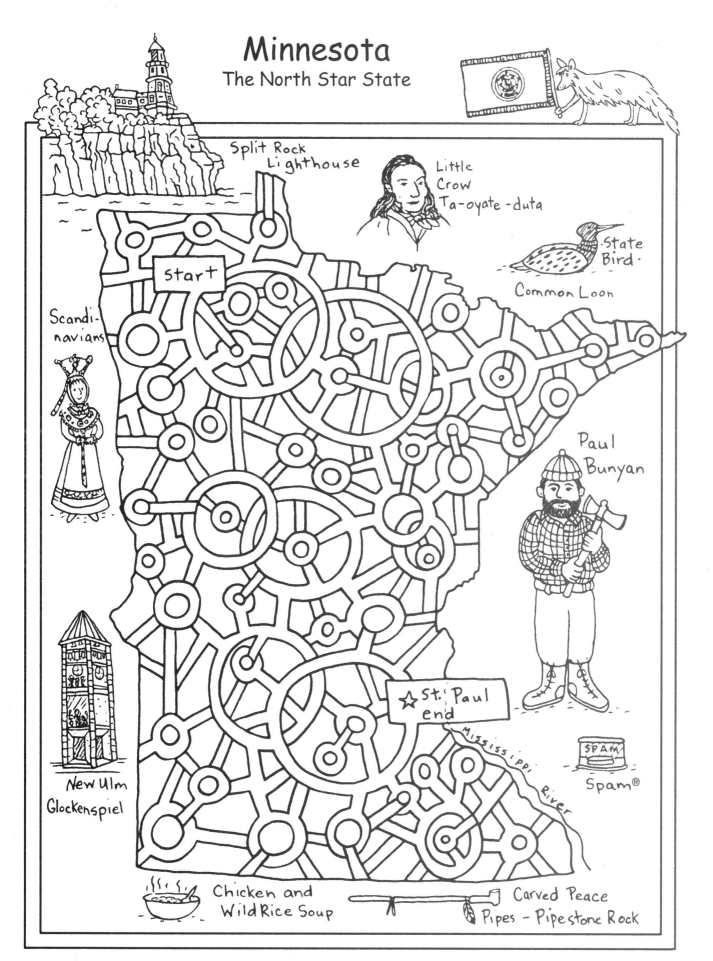

Split Rock Lighthouse

Little Crow Ta-oyate-duta

State Bird. Common Loon

Scandinavians

Start

Paul Bunyan

New Ulm Glockenspiel

St. Paul end

Mississippi River

Spam®

Chicken and Wild Rice Soup

Carved Peace Pipes - Pipestone Rock

# Mississippi
## The Magnolia State

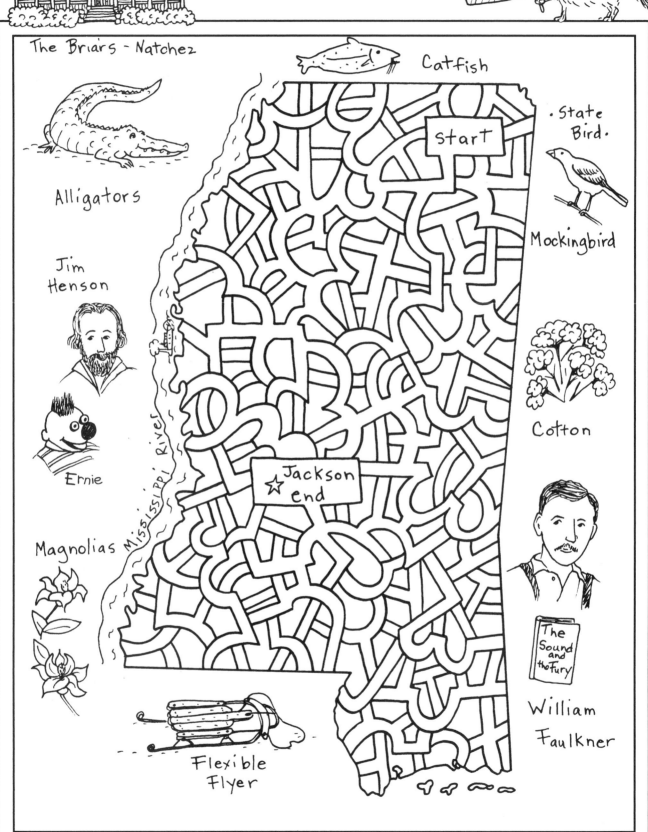

The Briars - Natchez

Catfish

Alligators

Start

. State Bird .

Mockingbird

Jim Henson

Ernie

Cotton

Magnolias

Mississippi River

Jackson end

The Sound and the Fury

William Faulkner

Flexible Flyer

24

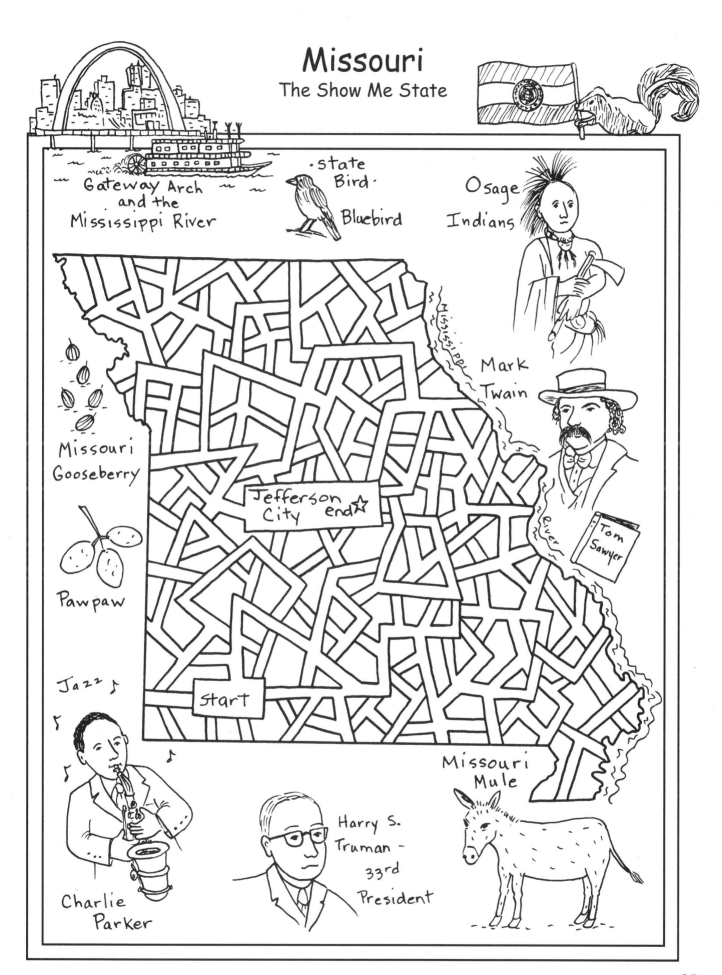

# Missouri
## The Show Me State

Gateway Arch and the Mississippi River

state Bird. Bluebird

Osage Indians

Mark Twain

Tom Sawyer

Missouri Gooseberry

Pawpaw

Jefferson City end ☆

Start

Jazz ♪

Charlie Parker

Harry S. Truman - 33rd President

Missouri Mule

# Montana
## The Treasure State

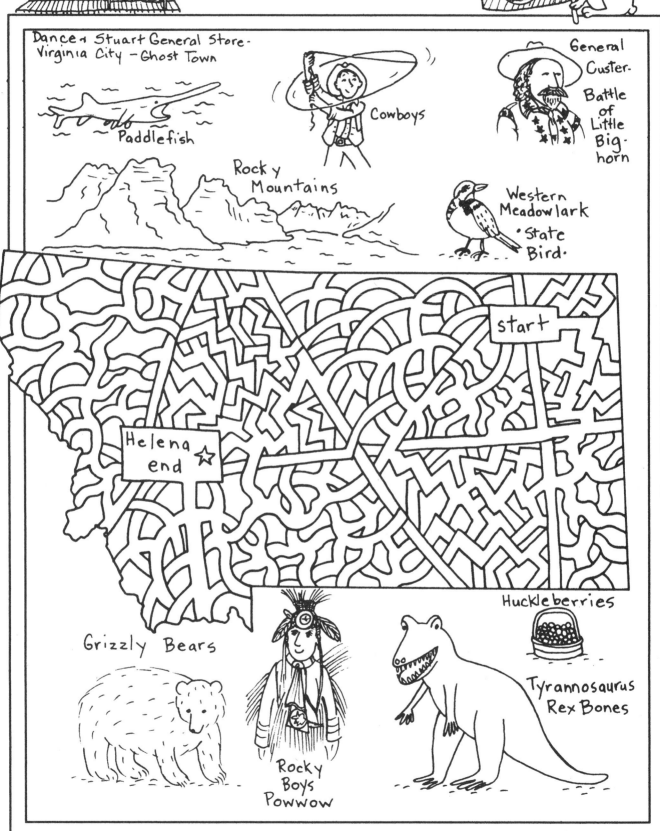

Dance + Stuart General Store -
Virginia City — Ghost Town

Paddlefish

Cowboys

General
Custer.
Battle
of
Little
Big-
horn

Rocky
Mountains

Western
Meadowlark
· State
Bird ·

start

Helena
end

Huckleberries

Grizzly Bears

Rocky
Boys
Powwow

Tyrannosaurus
Rex Bones

# Nebraska
## The Cornhusker State

Homestead National Monument of America

Corn

·State Bird·

Western Meadowlark

Cornbread

Carhenge

Sandhill Cranes

start

Chimney Rock

Lincoln end ☆

steaks

Buffalo Bill Cody

Dr. Susan LaFlesche Picotte

Tornadoes

Toadstool Park

Corn Dogs

# Nevada
## The Silver State

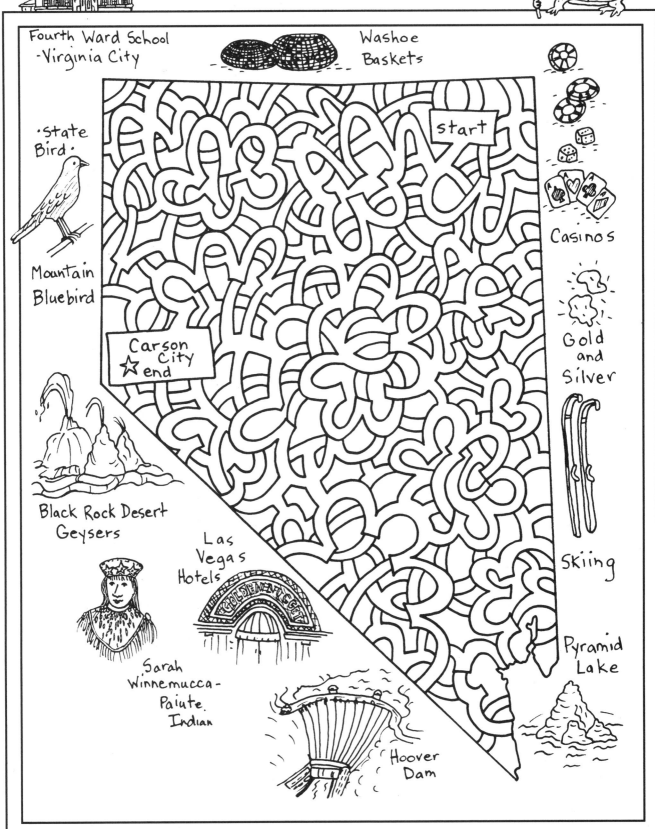

Fourth Ward School
-Virginia City

Washoe
Baskets

·state
Bird·

Mountain
Bluebird

start

Casinos

Gold
and
Silver

Carson
City
☆ end

Black Rock Desert
Geysers

Las
Vegas
Hotels

Skiing

Sarah
Winnemucca-
Paiute.
Indian

Hoover
Dam

Pyramid
Lake

# New Hampshire
## The Granite State

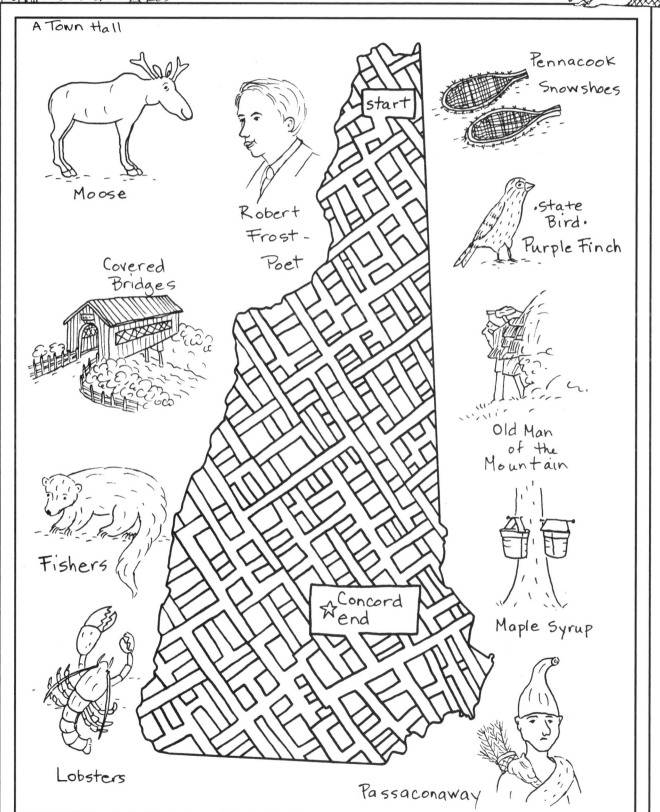

A Town Hall

Moose

Robert Frost - Poet

Covered Bridges

Fishers

Lobsters

start

Pennacook Snowshoes

·State Bird·
Purple Finch

Old Man of the Mountain

Maple Syrup

Concord
end

Passaconaway

# New Jersey
## The Garden State

Cape May

Lenni Lenape

Dugout Canoes

Miss America Pageant- Atlantic City

Molly Pitcher

Monopoly

BalticAve Rent

PARK PLACE Rent

Albert Einstein

$E = mc^2$

State Bird

Eastern Goldfinch

Thomas Edison

Blackbeard's Cave

Salt Water Taffy

DINER

Diners

Trenton ☆ end

Start

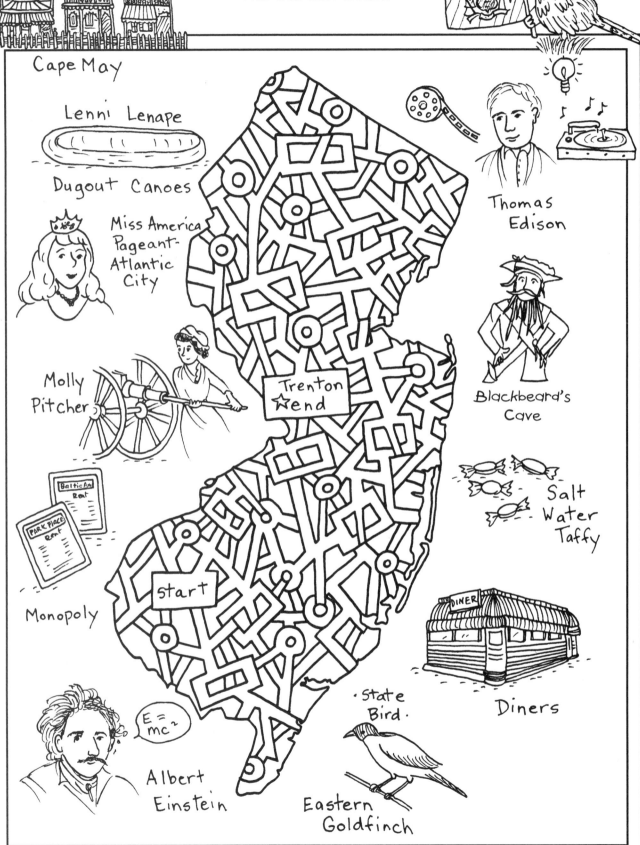

# New Mexico
## The Land of Enchantment

Taos Pueblo

Pueblo Indian Pottery

Shiprock

Weavings

Dried Hot Peppers

Petroglyphs

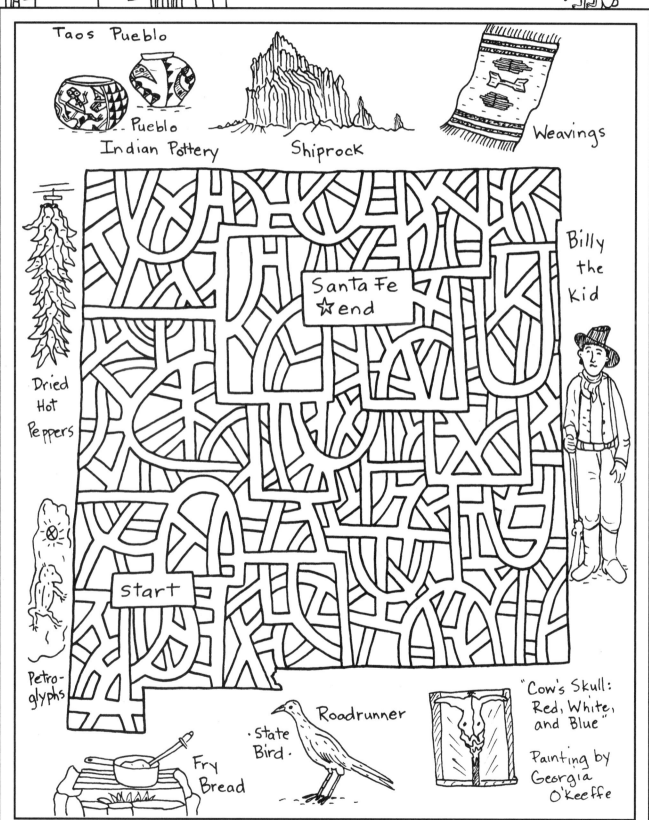

Santa Fe ☆ end

Billy the Kid

Start

Fry Bread

Roadrunner
·State Bird.

"Cow's Skull: Red, White, and Blue"

Painting by Georgia O'Keeffe

# New York
## The Empire State

Ellis Island

Iroquois Indian Mask

Coney Island

Hot Dogs

Empire State Building

State Bird.

Apples

Eastern Bluebird

start

Albany end

Grapes

Rip Van Winkle

Sleepy Hollow

Jackie Robinson

statue of Liberty

Niagara Falls

# North Carolina
## The Tar Heel State

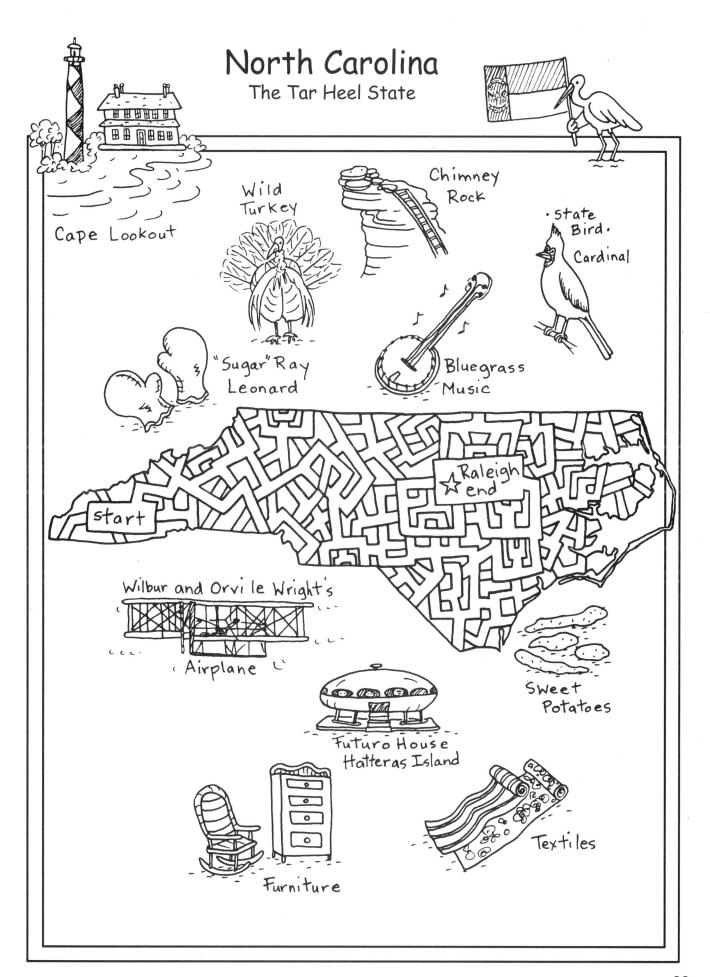

Cape Lookout

Wild Turkey

Chimney Rock

· state Bird · Cardinal

"Sugar" Ray Leonard

Bluegrass Music

start

☆ Raleigh end

Wilbur and Orville Wright's

Airplane

Futuro House Hatteras Island

Sweet Potatoes

Furniture

Textiles

# North Dakota
## The Peace Garden State

International Peace Garden

Theodore Roosevelt National Park

Honey

World's Largest Tin Family

Wheat

Start

Bismarck ☆ end

Prairie Dogs

World's Largest Buffalo

Earth Hidatsa Houses

·State Bird·

Meadowlark

Lakotas

# Ohio
## The Buckeye State

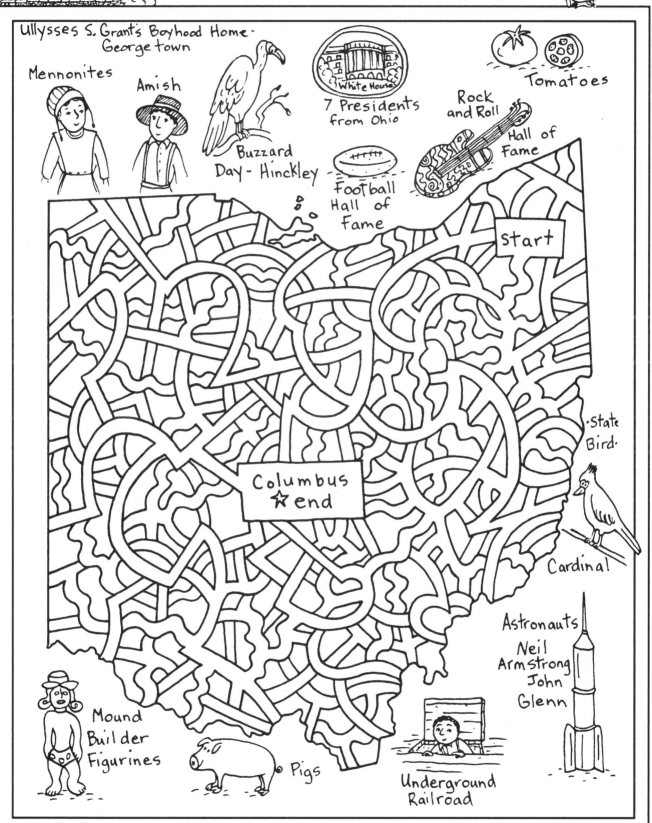

Ullysses S. Grant's Boyhood Home - Georgetown

Mennonites

Amish

Buzzard Day - Hinckley

7 Presidents from Ohio

Football Hall of Fame

Rock and Roll Hall of Fame

Tomatoes

Start

State Bird

Columbus ☆ end

Cardinal

Astronauts
Neil Armstrong
John Glenn

Mound Builder Figurines

Pigs

Underground Railroad

# Oklahoma
## The Sooner State

Downtown Guthrie

Cherokee Winter House

Will Rogers

Land Rushes

Tornadoes

Scissor-Tailed Flycather
·State Bird.

"Sooner's" Homestead

start

Buffalo Soldiers

☆ Oklahoma City
end

Chicken-Fried Steak

Cowboy Hall of Fame

Woody Guthrie

# Oregon
## The Beaver State

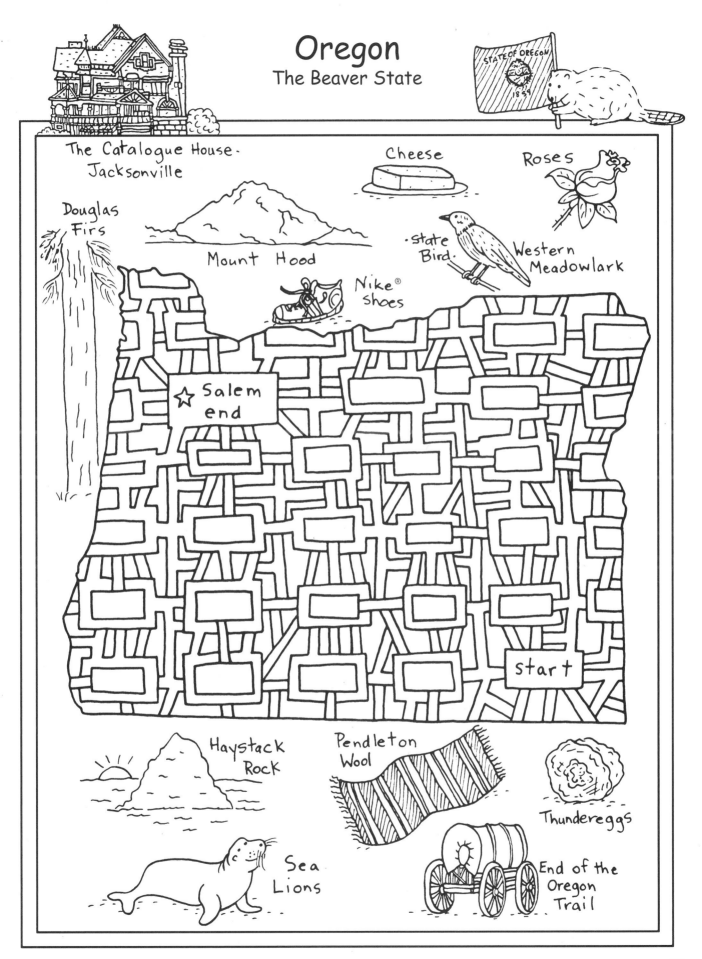

The Catalogue House - Jacksonville

Cheese

Roses

Douglas Firs

Mount Hood

State Bird.

Western Meadowlark

Nike® shoes

☆ Salem end

start

Haystack Rock

Pendleton Wool

Thundereggs

Sea Lions

End of the Oregon Trail

STATE OF OREGON 1859

# Pennsylvania
## The Keystone State

Independence Hall

Liberty Bell

Ben Franklin

Groundhog Day

Chocolate

Fossils · Trilobites

·State Bird·

Ruffled Grouse

Start

Harrisburg ☆ end

Amish

Mr. Rogers

Declaration of Independence

Lappawinsoe - Delaware Chief

# Rhode Island
## The Ocean State

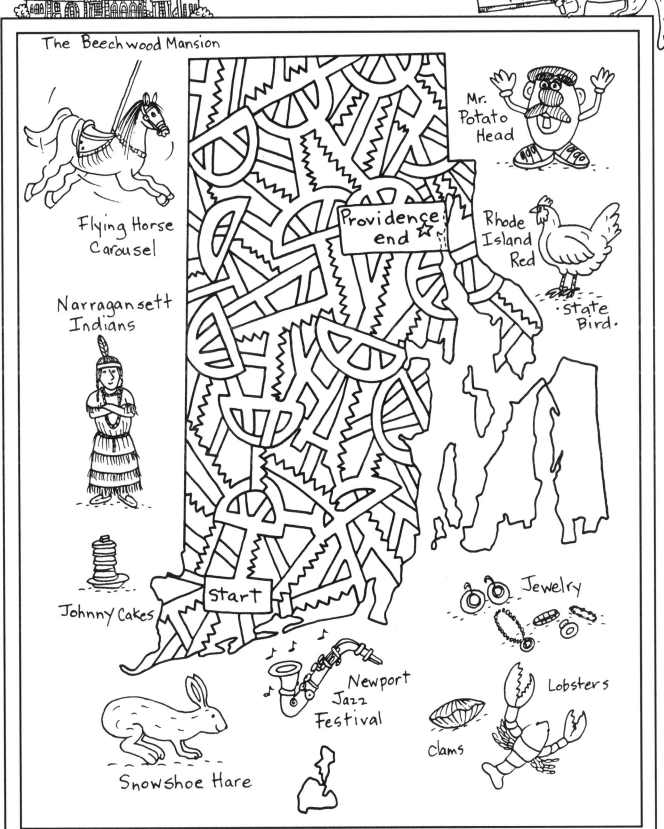

The Beechwood Mansion

Flying Horse Carousel

Narragansett Indians

Johnny Cakes

Snowshoe Hare

Mr. Potato Head

Rhode Island Red
·State Bird.

Providence end

Start

Newport Jazz Festival

Jewelry

Clams

Lobsters

# South Carolina
## The Palmetto State

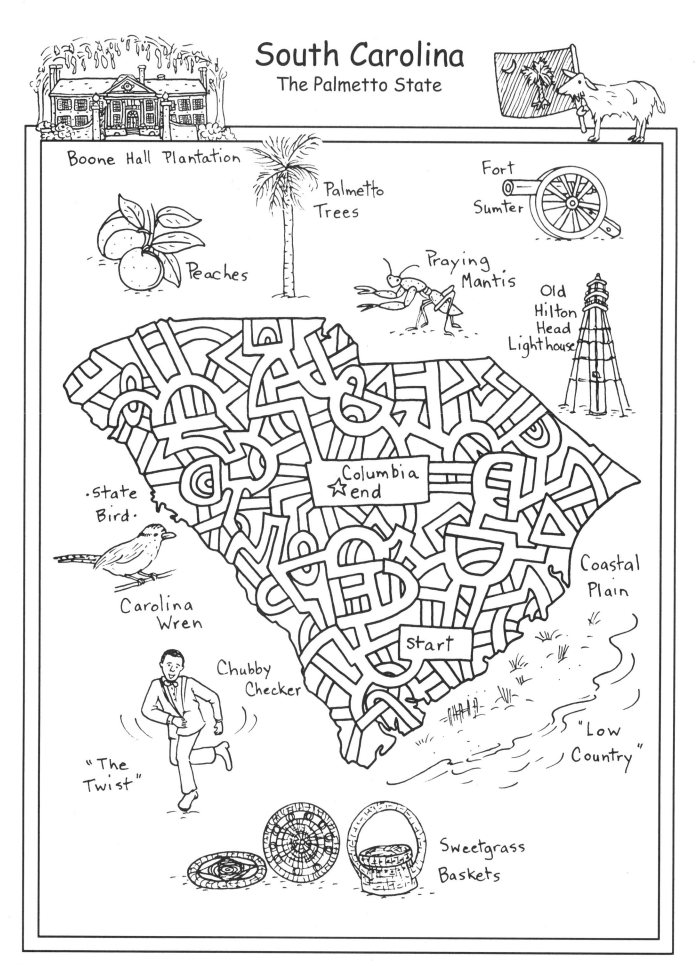

Boone Hall Plantation

Peaches

Palmetto Trees

Fort Sumter

Praying Mantis

Old Hilton Head Lighthouse

.State Bird.

Columbia ☆ end

Carolina Wren

Coastal Plain

Chubby Checker

Start

"The Twist"

"Low Country"

Sweetgrass Baskets

# South Dakota
## The Mount Rushmore State

Corn Palace

Deadwood

Wild Bill Hickok

Sitting Bull

Calamity Jane

Mount Rushmore

"Soddies" – the Sod Homes of "Sodbusters"

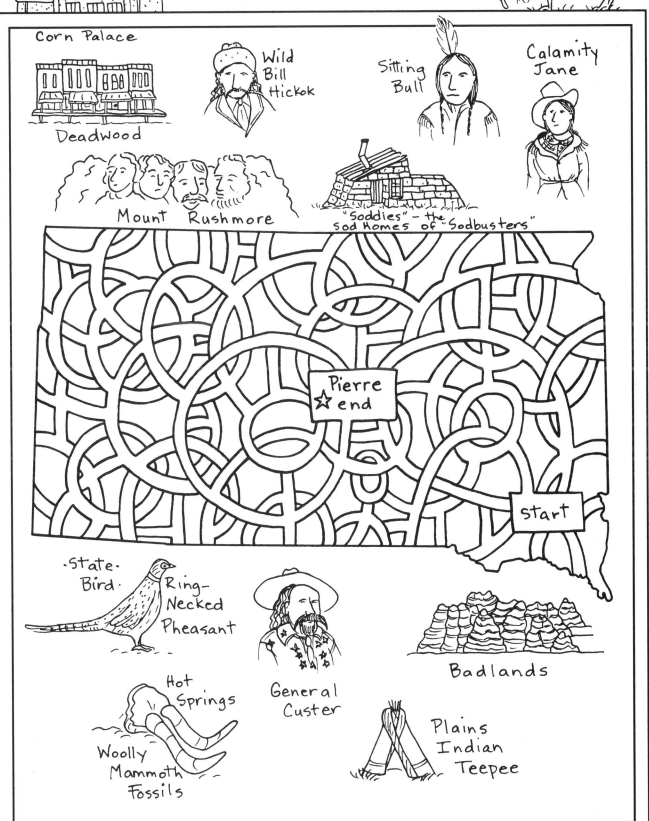

Pierre
★ end

Start

·State· Bird·
Ring-Necked Pheasant

Hot Springs

Woolly Mammoth Fossils

General Custer

Badlands

Plains Indian Teepee

# Tennessee
## The Volunteer State

Ryman Auditorium
-Former Home of
The Grand Ole Opry

Fried Green
Tomatoes

Beale
Street
Music

B B KING'S BLUES CLUB

Dolly
Parton

Pinson Mounds

Tennessee
Walking
Horse

Mississippi River

Nashville
☆end

Start

·state
Bird·
Mockingbird

Elvis
Presley

Tennessee
Coneflower

Davy
Crockett

Great Smoky
Mountains

# Texas
## The Lone Star State

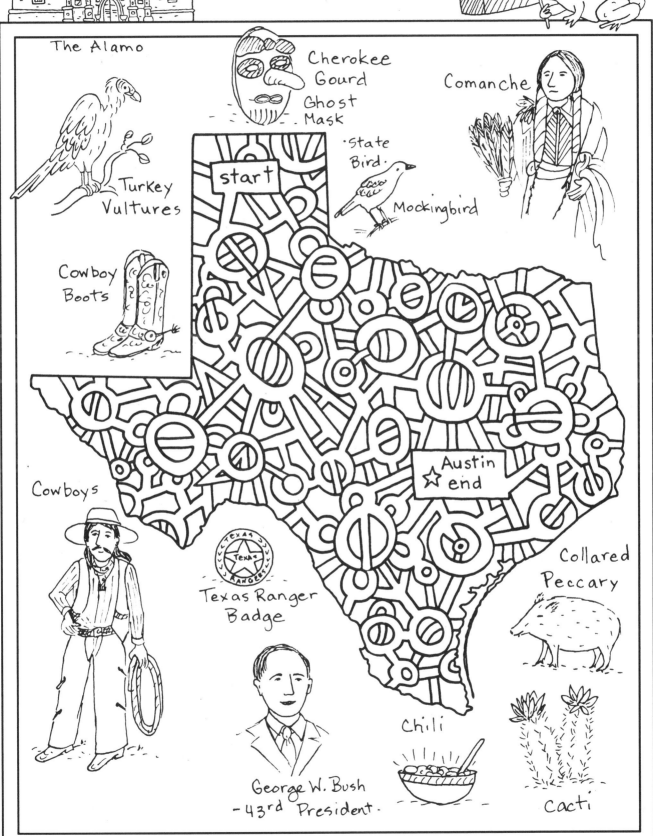

The Alamo

Cherokee Gourd Ghost Mask

Comanche

Turkey Vultures

State Bird.

start

Mockingbird

Cowboy Boots

Austin
☆ end

Cowboys

Collared Peccary

Texas Ranger Badge

Chili

George W. Bush
-43rd President.

Cacti

# Utah
## The Beehive State

Mormon Temple

Hoodoos-Rock. Formations

Four Corners Marker

Brigham Young

Anasazi Pottery

Bryce Canyon

Salt Lake City end

California Gull · State Bird ·

Newspaper Rock

start

The Great Salt Lake

# Vermont
## The Green Mountain State

The Old Round Church

Cheese

Ice Cream

Calvin Coolidge · 30th US-President

Hermit Thrush

·State Bird·

Covered Bridges

Montpelier ☆ end

Skiing

Ethan Allen

Maple Syrup

Fall Colors

Start

Dairy

# Virginia
## The Old Dominion State

Mount Vernon-
George Washington's
Home

Virginia
Peanuts

Virginia
Oysters

Cardinal

Natural
Bridge

Blue
Ridge
Mountains

· state
Bird ·

Richmond
end

start

River
Otters

George
Washington

Great
Blue
Heron

The Fife
and Drum

# Washington
## The Evergreen State

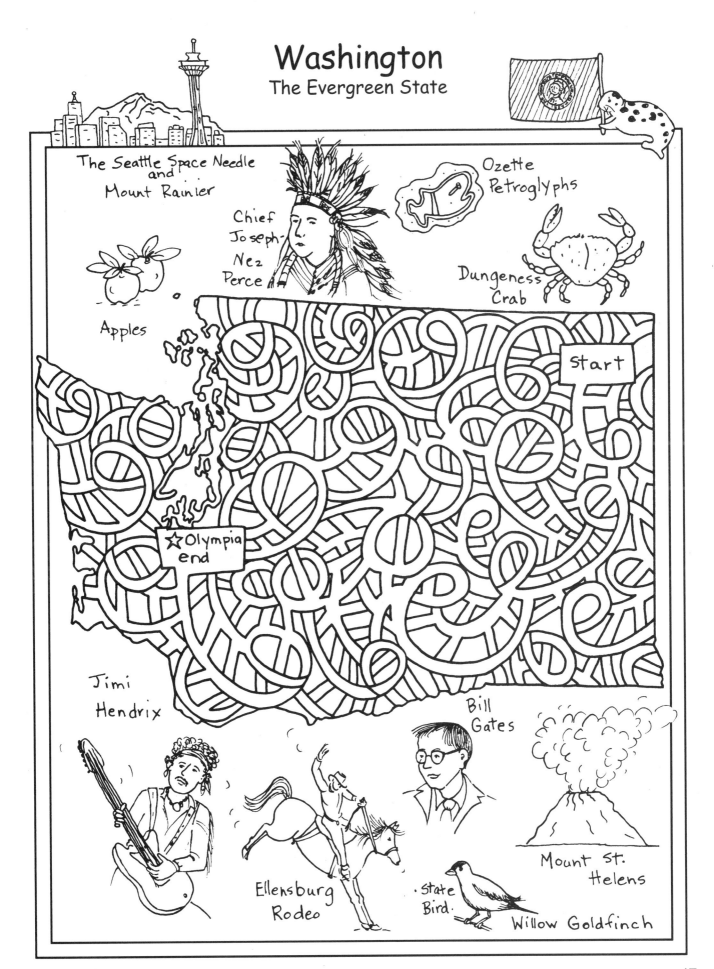

The Seattle Space Needle
and
Mount Rainier

Apples

Chief Joseph-
Nez Perce

Ozette Petroglyphs

Dungeness Crab

Start

☆Olympia
end

Jimi Hendrix

Ellensburg Rodeo

Bill Gates

State Bird.

Mount St. Helens

Willow Goldfinch

# West Virginia
## The Mountain State

Jefferson County Courthouse - Where John Brown Stood Trial

Folk Music

Quilts

Apple Butter Festival

Daniel Boone

Spruce Knob Forest

Golden Delicious Apples

Start

Charleston end ☆

Moundsville

state Bird

Cardinal

Glass Blowing

Folk Art

Appalachian Mountains

Philippi Bridge
Oldest and Longest Bridge in West Virginia

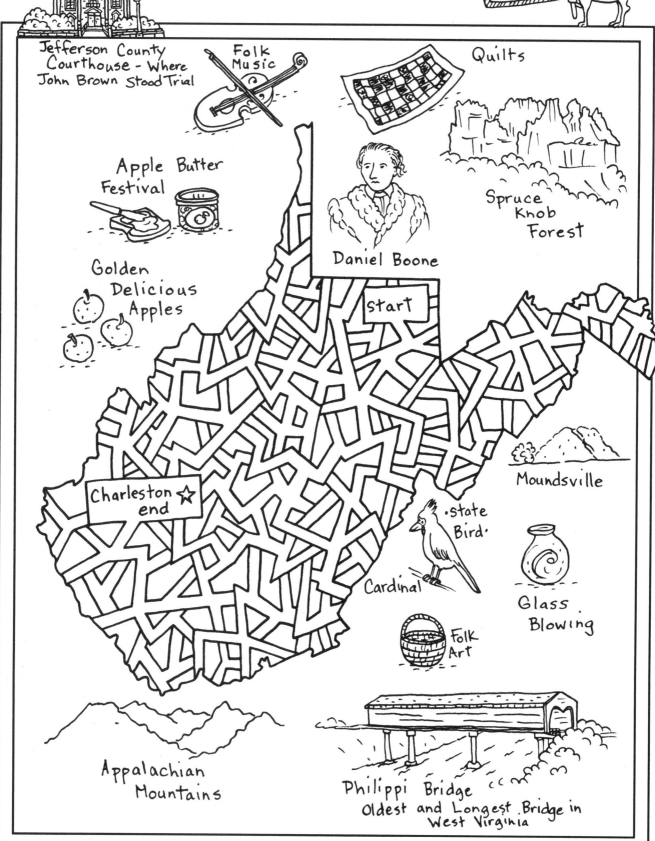

# Wisconsin
## The Badger State

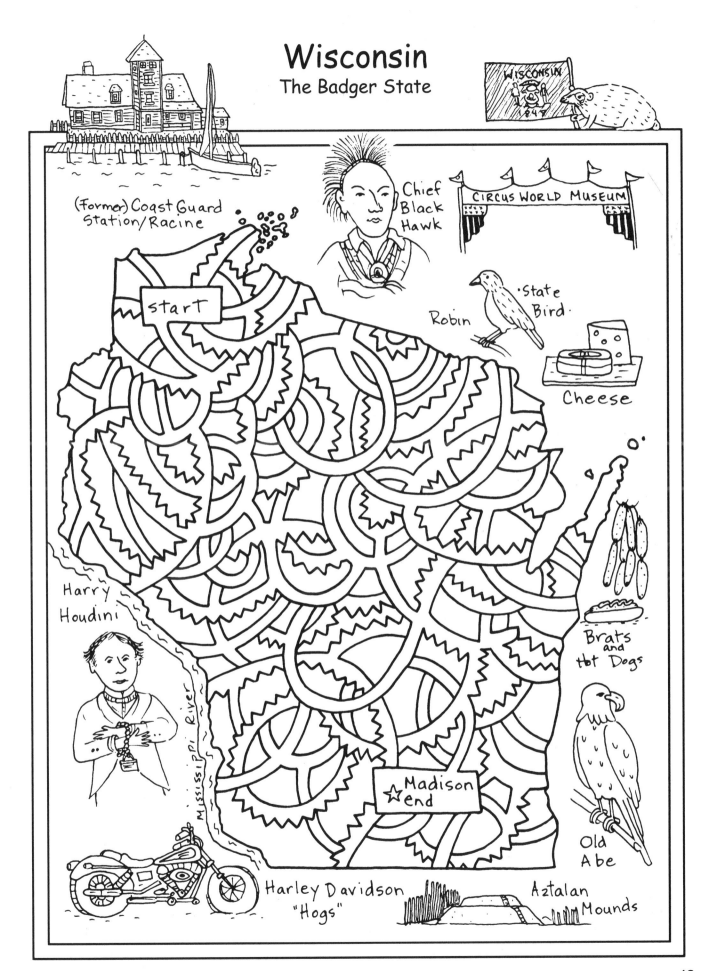

WISCONSIN 1848

(Former) Coast Guard Station/Racine

Chief Black Hawk

CIRCUS WORLD MUSEUM

Robin · State Bird ·

Cheese

start

Harry Houdini

Mississippi River

Brats and Hot Dogs

☆Madison end

Old Abe

Harley Davidson "Hogs"

Aztalan Mounds

# Wyoming
## The Cowboy State
## [also] The Equality State

St. Stephen's Mission

Ten-Gallon Hat

The Mythical "Jackalope"

Old Faithful Geyser

Ice Fishing

start

Cheyenne end ☆

Devils Tower

Cowboys

·state Bird·
Meadowlark

Red Cloud- Sioux Chief

# Solutions

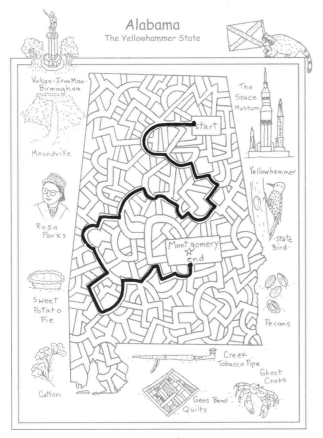

### Alabama
The Yellowhammer State

**page 1**

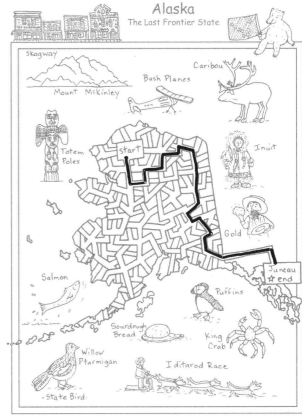

### Alaska
The Last Frontier State

**page 2**

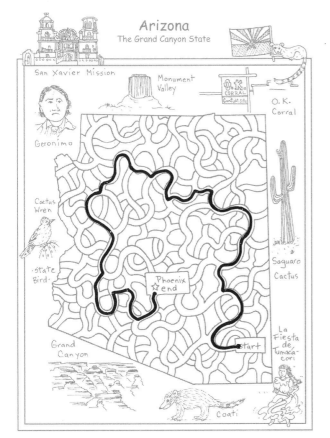

### Arizona
The Grand Canyon State

**page 3**

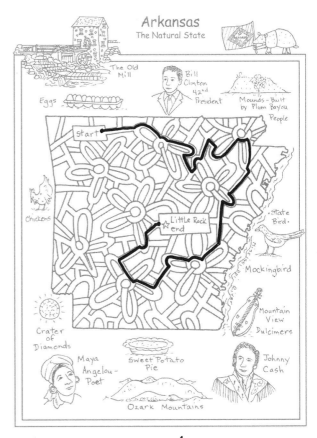

### Arkansas
The Natural State

**page 4**

## California
The Golden State

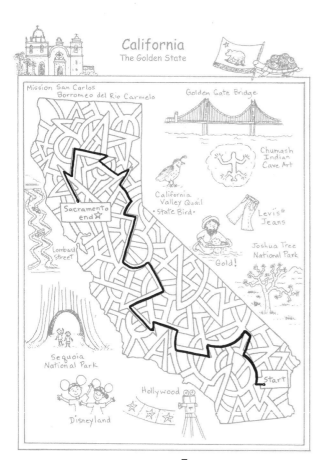

Mission San Carlos Borromeo del Rio Carmelo

Golden Gate Bridge

Chumash Indian Cave Art

California Valley Quail · State Bird ·

Sacramento end ☆

Levis® Jeans

Lombard Street

Gold!

Joshua Tree National Park

Sequoia National Park

Hollywood

Disneyland

**page 5**

## Colorado
The Centennial State

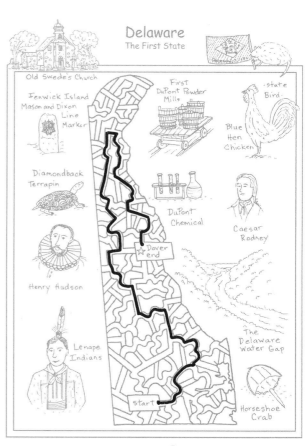

Bent's Old Fort

The Crow

U.S. Mint

Rocky Mountains

Jim Beckwourth

Miner's Burro

Denver end ☆

Start

Anasazi Cliff Palace

Tea

Lark Bunting

· State Bird ·

Baby Doe Tabor

Chief Ouray

Ghost Towns

**page 6**

## Connecticut
The Constitution State

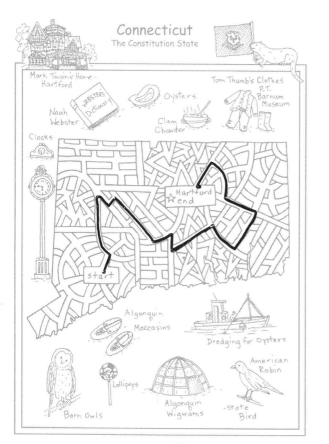

Mark Twain's Home Hartford

Tom Thumb's Clothes P.T. Barnum Museum

Noah Webster

WEBSTER'S Dictionary

Oysters

Clam Chowder

Clocks

Hartford end ☆

Start

Algonquin Moccasins

Dredging for Oysters

American Robin

Barn Owls

Lollipops

Algonquin Wigwams

· State Bird ·

**page 7**

## Delaware
The First State

Old Swede's Church

Fenwick Island Mason and Dixon Line Marker

First DuPont Powder Mills

· State Bird ·

Blue Hen Chicken

Diamondback Terrapin

DuPont Chemical

Caesar Rodney

Dover end ☆

Henry Hudson

Lenape Indians

The Delaware Water Gap

Start

Horseshoe Crab

**page 8**

**page 9**

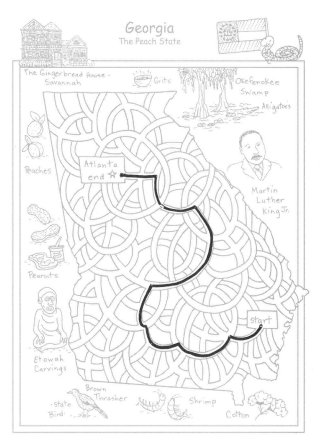

**page 10**

**page 11**

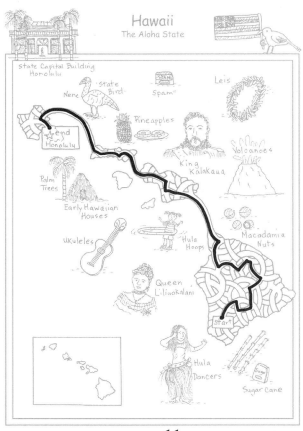

**page 12**

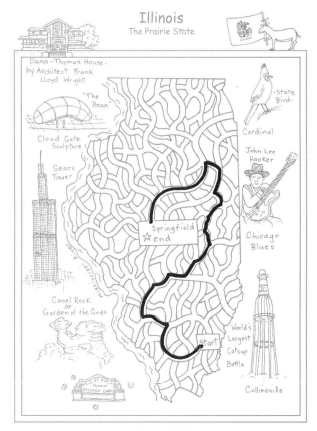

## Illinois
### The Prairie State

Dana-Thomas House by Architect Frank Lloyd Wright

"The Bean"

Cloud Gate Sculpture

Sears Tower

Camel Rock at Garden of the Gods

•State Bird•
Cardinal

John Lee Hooker

Chicago Blues

World's Largest Catsup Bottle

Springfield ☆ end

start

Collinsville

**page 13**

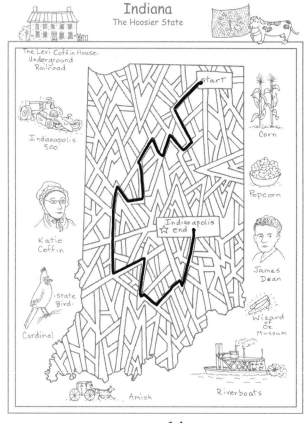

## Indiana
### The Hoosier State

The Levi Coffin House Underground Railroad

Indianapolis 500

Katie Coffin

•State Bird•
Cardinal

start

Corn

Popcorn

James Dean

Wizard of Oz Museum

Indianapolis ☆ end

Amish

Riverboats

**page 14**

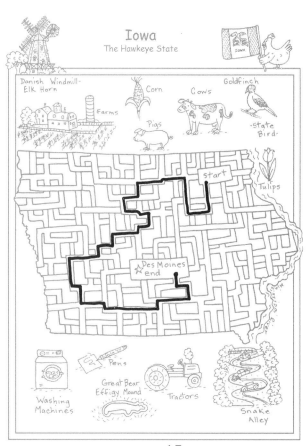

## Iowa
### The Hawkeye State

Danish Windmill Elk Horn

Farms

Corn

Pigs

Cows

Goldfinch

•State Bird•

Tulips

Start

Des Moines ☆ end

Washing Machines

Pens

Great Bear Effigy Mound

Tractors

Snake Alley

**page 15**

## Kansas
### The Sunflower State

1880's Dodge City Boot Hill Museum

Amelia Earhart

Airplanes

Sunflowers

World's Largest Ball of Twine

Cawker City

•State Bird•
Meadowlark

start

Topeka ☆ end

Rock City

International Pancake Derby

Russell Stover Chocolates

Tornadoes

Wizard of Oz

**page 16**

54

### Kentucky
The Bluegrass State

Calumet Horse Farm

Abraham Lincoln

Daniel Boone

The Hatfields and McCoys

Crafts

Frankfort ☆end

start

First Cheeseburger

state Bird

Kentucky Cardinal

Shaker Furniture

Kentucky Derby

Mammoth Caves

Bluegrass Music

**page 17**

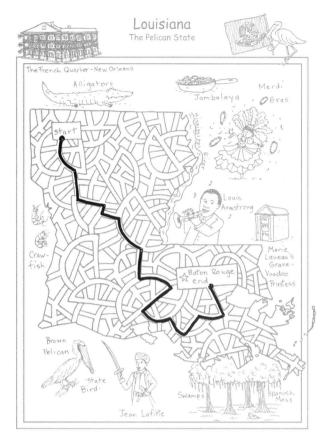

### Louisiana
The Pelican State

The French Quarter-New Orleans

Alligators

Jambalaya

Mardi Gras

start

Louis Armstrong

Marie Laveau's Grave-Voodoo Priestess

Cray-fish

☆Baton Rouge end

Brown Pelican

·state Bird·

Jean Lafitte

Swamps

Spanish Moss

**page 18**

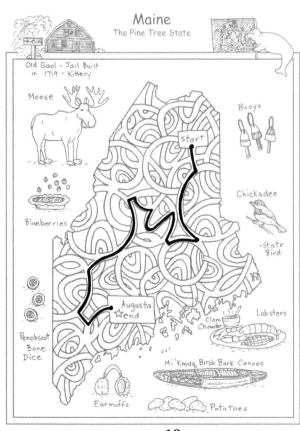

### Maine
The Pine Tree State

Old Gaol - Jail Built in 1719 - Kittery

Moose

Buoys

start

Chickadee

Blueberries

·State Bird·

Augusta ☆end

Penobscot Bone Dice

Clam Chowder

Lobsters

Mi'Kmaq Birch Bark Canoes

Earmuffs

Potatoes

**page 19**

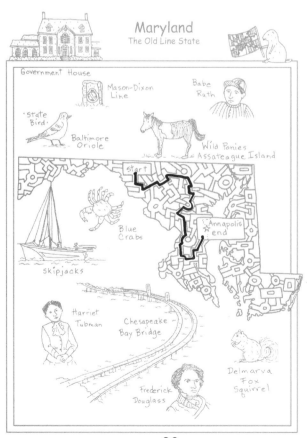

### Maryland
The Old Line State

Government House

Mason-Dixon Line

Babe Ruth

·State Bird·

Baltimore Oriole

Wild Ponies Assateague Island

start

Blue Crabs

☆Annapolis end

Skipjacks

Harriet Tubman

Chesapeake Bay Bridge

Delmarva Fox Squirrel

Frederick Douglass

**page 20**

**Massachusetts**
The Bay State

Lobster Pot Restaurant
Cape Cod

Boston Common

Dr. Seuss "The Cat in the Hat"

John F. Kennedy 35th President

Cranberry Bogs

Plymouth Rock

Boston end ☆

start

Chickadee · state Bird·

The First Basketball

Scallops

Wampanoags' Canoes

Lake Chargoggagoggmanchaugagoggchaubunagungamaug

Yahtzee®

Scrabble®

(Hasbro) Milton Bradley Games

Pilgrims

**page 21**

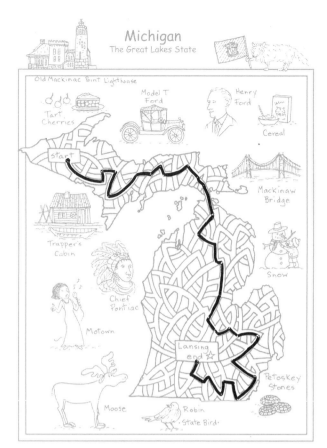

**Michigan**
The Great Lakes State

Old Mackinac Point Lighthouse

Tart Cherries

Model T Ford

Henry Ford

Cereal

start

Mackinaw Bridge

Trapper's Cabin

Chief Pontiac

Snow

Motown

Lansing end ☆

Petoskey Stones

Moose

Robin · State Bird·

**page 22**

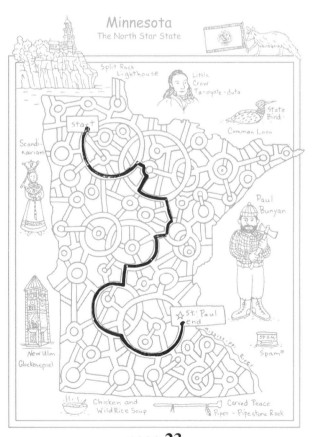

**Minnesota**
The North Star State

Split Rock Lighthouse

Little Crow Ta-oyate-duta

· State Bird·

Common Loon

start

Scandinavian

Paul Bunyan

New Ulm Glockenspiel

St. Paul end ☆

Spam®

Chicken and Wild Rice Soup

Carved Peace Pipes - Pipestone Rock

**page 23**

**Mississippi**
The Magnolia State

The Briars - Natchez

Catfish

· State Bird·

Alligators

start

Mockingbird

Jim Henson

Cotton

Ernie

Jackson end ☆

Magnolias

Mississippi River

William Faulkner

The Sound and the Fury

Flexible Flyer

**page 24**

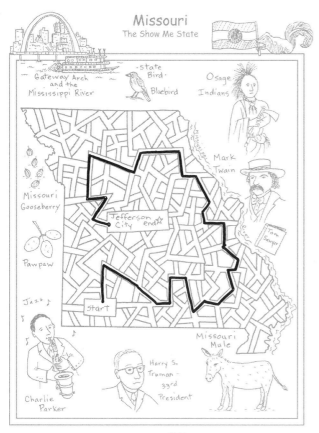

**page 25**

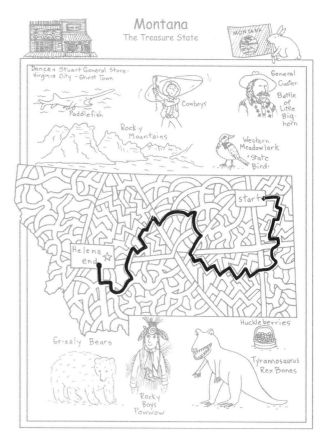

**page 26**

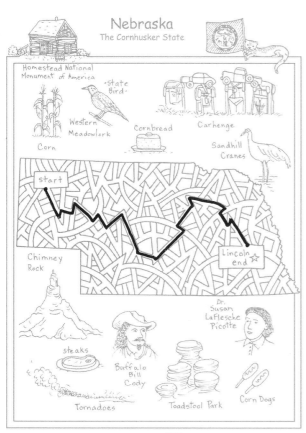

**page 27**

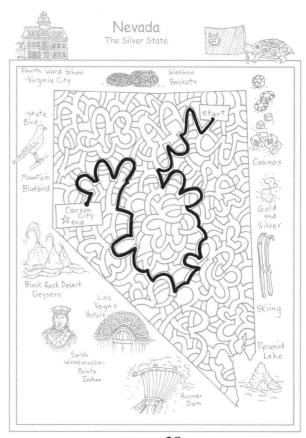

**page 28**

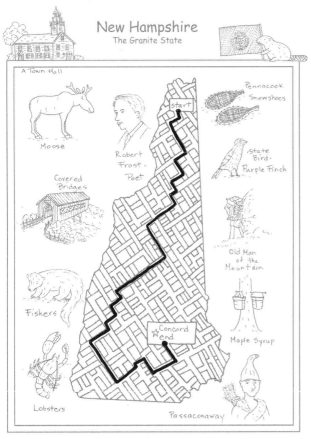

### New Hampshire
The Granite State

A Town Hall

Moose

Robert Frost - Poet

Covered Bridges

Fishers

Lobsters

start

Concord end

Pennacook Snowshoes

State Bird - Purple Finch

Old Man of the Mountain

Maple Syrup

Passaconaway

**page 29**

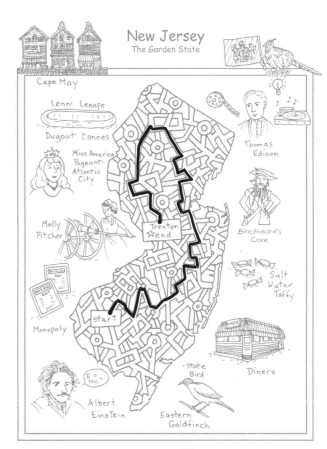

### New Jersey
The Garden State

Cape May

Lenni Lenape

Dugout Canoes

Miss America Pageant - Atlantic City

Molly Pitcher

Monopoly

Albert Einstein

$E = mc^2$

start

Trenton end

Eastern Goldfinch

State Bird

Thomas Edison

Blackbeard's Cove

Salt Water Taffy

Diners

**page 30**

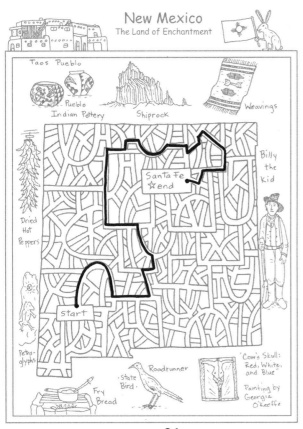

### New Mexico
The Land of Enchantment

Taos Pueblo

Pueblo Indian Pottery

Shiprock

Weavings

Dried Hot Peppers

Santa Fe end

Billy the Kid

start

Petroglyphs

Fry Bread

Roadrunner

State Bird

Cow's Skull: Red, White, and Blue

Painting by Georgia O'Keeffe

**page 31**

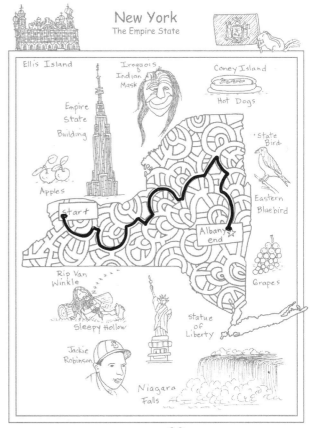

### New York
The Empire State

Ellis Island

Iroquois Indian Mask

Coney Island

Hot Dogs

Empire State Building

Apples

start

Albany end

Rip Van Winkle

Sleepy Hollow

Jackie Robinson

Statue of Liberty

Niagara Falls

State Bird

Eastern Bluebird

Grapes

**page 32**

## North Carolina
### The Tar Heel State

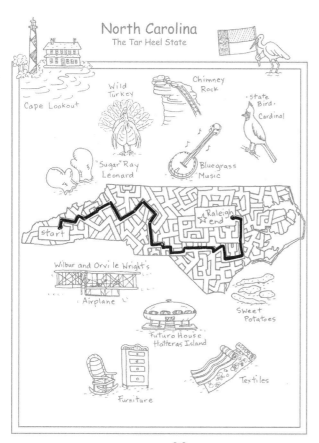

Cape Lookout

Wild Turkey

Chimney Rock

·State Bird·
Cardinal

"Sugar" Ray Leonard

Bluegrass Music

start

★ Raleigh end

Wilbur and Orville Wright's

Airplane

Sweet Potatoes

Futuro House Hatteras Island

Furniture

Textiles

**page 33**

## North Dakota
### The Peace Garden State

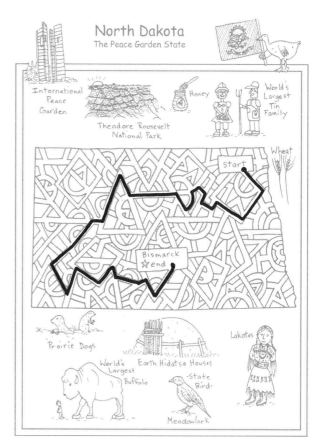

International Peace Garden

Theodore Roosevelt National Park

Honey

World's Largest Tin Family

Wheat

start

Bismarck ★ end

Prairie Dogs

World's Largest Buffalo

Earth Hidatsa Houses

·State Bird·
Meadowlark

Lakotas

**page 34**

## Ohio
### The Buckeye State

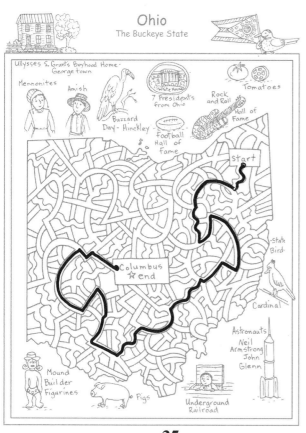

Ullysses S. Grant's Boyhood Home· Georgetown

Mennonites

Amish

Buzzard Day·Hinckley

7 Presidents from Ohio

Football Hall of Fame

Rock and Roll Hall of Fame

Tomatoes

Start

·State Bird·

Columbus ★ end

Cardinal

Mound Builder Figurines

Pigs

Underground Railroad

Astronauts Neil Armstrong John Glenn

**page 35**

## Oklahoma
### The Sooner State

Downtown Guthrie

Cherokee Winter House

Tornadoes

Will Rogers

Land Rushes

Scissor-Tailed Flycatcher

·State Bird·

"Sooner's" Homestead

start

Buffalo Soldiers

Oklahoma ★ end City

Chicken-Fried Steak

Cowboy Hall of Fame

Woody Guthrie

**page 36**

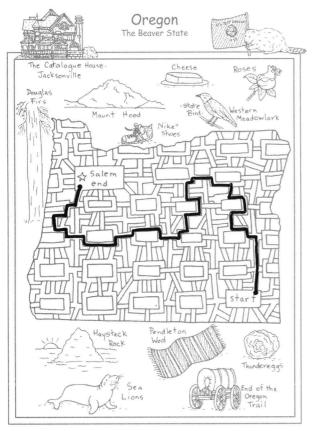

## Oregon
### The Beaver State

The Catalogue House - Jacksonville

Douglas Firs

Cheese

Roses

Mount Hood

Nike® shoes

·State Bird·
Western Meadowlark

☆ Salem end

Start

Haystack Rock

Pendleton Wool

Thundereggs

Sea Lions

End of the Oregon Trail

**page 37**

## Pennsylvania
### The Keystone State

Independence Hall

Liberty Bell

Chocolate

Ben Franklin

Groundhog Day

·State Bird·
Ruffled Grouse

Fossils

Trilobites

☆ Harrisburg end

Start

Amish

Declaration of Independence

Mr. Rogers

Lappawinsoe - Delaware Chief

**page 38**

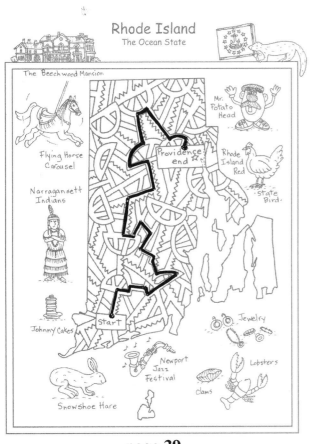

## Rhode Island
### The Ocean State

The Beechwood Mansion

Mr. Potato Head

Flying Horse Carousel

Providence end ☆

Rhode Island Red

·State Bird·

Narragansett Indians

Start

Johnny Cakes

Jewelry

Newport Jazz Festival

Lobsters

Snowshoe Hare

Clams

**page 39**

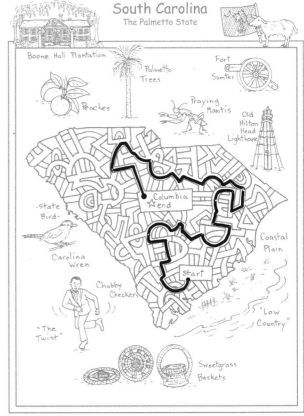

## South Carolina
### The Palmetto State

Boone Hall Plantation

Palmetto Trees

Fort Sumter

Peaches

Praying Mantis

Old Hilton Head Lighthouse

·State Bird·

Columbia end ☆

Carolina Wren

Start

Coastal Plain

Chubby Checkers

"The Twist"

"Low Country"

Sweetgrass Baskets

**page 40**

## South Dakota
### The Mount Rushmore State

Corn Palace
Deadwood
Wild Bill Hickok
Sitting Bull
Calamity Jane
Mount Rushmore
"Soddies" - the Sod Homes of the Sodbusters
·State Bird· Ring-Necked Pheasant
Hot Springs
Woolly Mammoth Fossils
General Custer
Plains Indian Teepee
Badlands
Pierre ☆ end
start

## Tennessee
### The Volunteer State

Ryman Auditorium -Former Home of The Grand Ole Opry
Dolly Parton
Fried Green Tomatoes
Beale Street Music
KINGS BLUES CLUB
Pinson Mounds
Tennessee Walking Horse
Mississippi R.
Nashville ☆ end
Start
·State Bird· Mockingbird
Elvis Presley
Tennessee Coneflower
Davy Crockett
Great Smoky Mountains

## Texas
### The Lone Star State

The Alamo
Turkey Vultures
Cowboy Boots
Cowboys
Cherokee Gourd Ghost Mask
·State Bird· Mockingbird
Comanche
start
Texas Ranger Badge
George W. Bush -43rd President·
Chili
Collared Peccary
Cacti
Austin ☆ end

## Utah
### The Beehive State

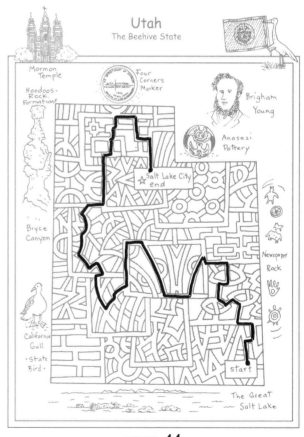

Mormon Temple
Hoodoos- Rock Formations
Four Corners Marker
Brigham Young
Anasazi Pottery
Bryce Canyon
Salt Lake City ☆ end
California Gull
·State Bird·
Newspaper Rock
start
The Great Salt Lake

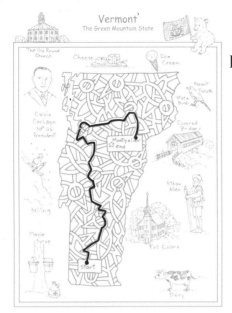

Vermont
The Green Mountain State

**page 45**

Virginia
The Old Dominion State

**page 46**

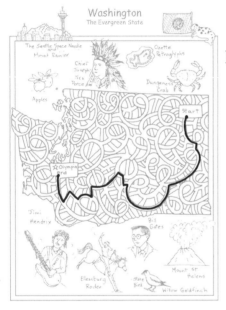

Washington
The Evergreen State

**page 47**

West Virginia
The Mountain State

**page 48**

Wisconsin
The Badger State

**page 49**

Wyoming
The Cowboy State
[also] The Equality State

**page 50**